CW00369591

40 Super Tips For Networking You & Your Business

quick & easy tips that you can implement today to build your business network - even if you're naturally shy

by Mathew Corner

Scorching Books

DISCLAIMER

This information in book is provided only to inform and entertain. Information is based on personal

experience and anecdotal evidence, and should not replace legal, financial, technical or other

professional advice. Time and success estimates are approximate and may vary widely based on user's

application of the materials, as well as the nature of the project. Use common sense. Readers assume full responsibility for use of the information in this book. The
author and publisher cannot be responsible for how this information is used or misused, or its effects on your business successes, finances, or... well, anything else.

Scorching Books™
1500A Lafayette Road, #143

Portsmouth, NH 03801 USA

Think "Long Term"

When networking, you need to remember that you are trying to build long term relationships for yourself and your business; the aim is not to gain anything in the short term.

This is due to the fact that short term success is an unrealistic expectation, and having short term goals as your motivation during networking could distract you from building strong relationships that will benefit you much more in the long term.

You may find that even though you are focused on building long term relationships, you still find one or two leads for short term success, and that is why thinking long term is more productive - you will not be disappointed if you don't find short term leads, but you may find some even while building long term relationships.

A short term mindset usually involves conduct which is contrary to effective networking, and you may find that you alienate some people with whom you could have built great long term relationships by trying too hard to gain short term results from them.

Focusing on building strong, long term relationships has the added advantage of regular business, as opposed to short term relationships that usually end in the short term as well.

The key to long term networking is to build strong relationships with people to show them that you and your business are trustworthy and that you are the first person they come to when they are in need of services that you can provide.

Have a Game Plan

Having a game plan means that you need to think about your goals before attending any functions where you intend to network.

You need to think about your goals and formulate a clearly defined strategy that you will employ to fulfill these goals, and the best way to do this is to write it all down so that you can visualize it when you need to put it into action.

Think about the results that you intend to achieve by networking at this specific function or party, and make sure that you are equipped with a plan of action that will help you to achieve these results in the most effective way possible.

Often when networking, you know who the important contacts are who you need to meet, and the best way to ensure that you don't miss anyone significant is to make a list of them all beforehand.

Knowing who you need to meet also gives you the chance to prepare your questions or offers before arriving at the function, so it would pay to plan and make sure that you know exactly what you want to say.

Be Sincere

One of the worst things you can do when networking is coming across as someone who is insincere, and this is one of the most common mistakes made by many people who are new to networking.

Nobody likes to feel like you are only talking to them because you want something from them, and this is why sincerity plays such a significant role in networking - you need to show a genuine interest in the people you meet.

The most common question you'll ask and be asked is 'what do you do?' or some variation of it, and when you are the one asking it, you need to be as sincere as possible, making the person feel like you are genuinely interested in what they do and are not asking merely for personal gain.

You also need to ensure that you are comfortable talking to people for the first time, because being uncomfortable or nervous when meeting someone can also make them feel that you have ulterior motives for speaking to them, and this could work against you.

Being sincere also means that you engage in a real conversation with someone before making any offers or making references to any formal or business relationships.

Interpersonal Skills

'Working the room' requires strong interpersonal skills on various levels, and the only way to improve your interpersonal skills is to practice and go on courses that are specifically tailored for the purpose of improving these skills.

When you work on improving your skills, you need to work on building more than just a single approach, such as a subtle approach or one that tackles the topic directly.

Learn about body language and how it plays a part in good communication, because this is one of the most important aspects of interpersonal skills, both in formal and informal interaction.

Many people have mannerisms or habits that they may or may not be aware of, and it is important that you make yourself aware of your own so that you do not do anything that may portray you in a negative light.

Finally, you need to learn to read people from the moment you start talking to them, because this will aid you in identifying the approach that you need to take when trying to establish a formal relationship or even just trying to figure out whether an individual could serve as an asset to you (or your business) or not.

Confidence

Confidence is one of your greatest assets when 'working the room' because it makes the people you meet feel like you know what you want and that you are reliable and trustworthy because of it.

Even the most nervous person can appear confident, so you need to remember that even if you feel nervous or slightly intimidated by the task at hand, you can still make yourself appear as though you are confident, and that's the important thing.

Confidence also shows through in your physical appearance, so you need to ensure that your attire and demeanor exudes as much confidence as it possibly can, while your style and tone of voice do the rest.

Being confident is so pivotal because people will not take you seriously if you do not have a confident disposition - they will either think you are unprofessional or that you are inexperienced, and you would not want to be thought of as either of these things.

Confidence not only shows through in how you say things or the way you talk, but also in what you say. This means that you should not in any way portray yourself negatively - ensure that you always highlight your most positive attributes and that you come across as someone who is sure of your abilities and of your ability to contribute to someone else's success.

Learn to Listen

Networking is all about building great relationships from the moment you say 'hello' and one of the most important skills you need to do this is the ability to listen - and listen well.

It is extremely easy to notice when someone is not really paying attention to what you're saying, and it is just as easy to fall into the error of asking questions and not really listening to what the person says in response - either because you think you already know the answer or because you aren't really that interested.

The problem with this is that if you do not

listen you will not only make the other person feel uncomfortable or alienate them in some way, but you may also miss some vital information that could have been beneficial to you either in a later conversation with this person, or at some point in the future.

Acquiring listening skills is not at all hard to do, but it may prove difficult to get out of the habit of not paying attention if you already suffer from this bad habit.

The key here is to ensure that you identify any flaws in your listening habits, and ensure that you correct them as soon as possible, and as accurately as you can before attending any functions and trying to network, because your first impression may be the only chance you get at establishing a relationship with someone.

Make Yourself an Asset

You need to become the asset of others when networking so that people can see that you are reliable and that it pays for them to have you as a good friend or associate.

One of the easiest ways to do this is to introduce your current associates to others who may be of some benefit to them, because this will not only show them that you are resourceful and beneficial as an associate, but it will also show prospective associates that it could benefit them to establish relations with you.

This is the best way to market yourself as a networking resource, and ensures that any associates you have will be eager to return the favor and introduce you to everyone they know, which is exactly what networking is all about.

By marketing yourself in this way, you may also find that people you might not have heard of will come up to you because they have heard of your good reputation, and this may further boost your prospects for good long term relationships with as many people as possible.

You should also be sure to treat everyone with the same degree of respect and courtesy, and be especially mindful of this in your approach towards people who are currently less successful than you are - at some point in the future they may become an invaluable asset to you.

Regular Contact

It is vitally important that you maintain regular contact with the people you meet, even if they cannot help you immediately.

Staying in touch also means ensuring that you stick to your promises in terms of returning phone calls or following up on anything that you said you would do, because the easiest way to lose the respect and confidences of an individual is to fail in doing things that you had promised to do.
One of the most important reasons why you need to ensure that you follow up with people and stay in contact regularly is the fact that you may need them at

some point, and you wouldn't want that to be the first time you contacted them since you met.

People will gladly assist you if you build a strong relationship with them over time, but if you just come to them in your time of need and the relationship does not exist due to negligence, it is very rare that you will find the assistance that you seek.

The key to staying in contact is getting to know people so that if you meet someone who may be able to help them, you can call them up and let them know, share information and in this way build up a strong networking relationship.

Do Not Fear Rejection

One of the greatest milestones when networking for the first time is to overcome the fear of rejection; a fear that causes a great impediment in the networking process.

The reason for this is that you need to network with people by being warm, friendly and courteous, you need to smile and shake hands firmly and with confidence, make eye contact and show an interest in the way the other person responds to your questions, and all of this can be extremely hard to do if you have a lingering fear of being rejected.

Rejection is a risk that comes naturally with the environment in which you will be networking; there are so many people in the room and each of them has their own ideals and etiquette, so it is only normal that not everyone will respond to you in the same way.

You need to make a conscious realization that rejection is a factor that you will have to risk in order to find the right people with whom you can network and build relationships, and you need to realize that it isn't the end of the world if you do end up being rejected a few times.

Extend the Network

Extending your network is all about being warm and sociable wherever you are.

Once you realize that you can network everywhere you go, you will truly be able to unlock the secrets of successful networking. Whether you are at a festival, a sports event or even a wedding, you should employ your networking tactics and reach out to anyone you come into contact with.

Many people think that corporate events or functions are the only place where they can network effectively and achieve success, but in thinking so they forget that the corporate personalities are also human beings who have their own social lives, families and friends, and it is not uncommon to come across great leads in the last place you would expect to.

To be successful in extending your network you need to show a genuine interest in people no matter where you go, because being alert in this way will open your mind and open your eyes to new paths in the corporate network that you may otherwise have missed, and this could mean the difference between success and failure.

Just as you would take into account various interpersonal factors at corporate functions, you need to employ all of the same strategies when trying to extend your network into the rest of your social life, and you will soon find that your network grows automatically as you go about your regular routine.

The Business Card

The business card is an essential networking tool for anyone who is serious about building up successful relationships with a vast number of people.

To make effective use of the business card, you need to become comfortable with giving your business card to people, and you need to find a comfortable way in which to lead up to handing it out, since you cannot simply walk around the room handing them out to every second person you see.

It is quite common for people to part ways by sharing contact details before saying goodbye, and this is the easiest way for you to make use of your business cards. However, you may also find that at some point you will come across someone who is interested in services that you have to offer, and at this point you may also offer them your business card.

The key is to use your judgment as to when would be the appropriate time to exchange contact information with someone, because it shouldn't be a forced issue, but something that comes naturally either at the point of parting ways or at an appropriate time during conversation.

The only way to master the way you deliver your business card is to practice doing it as much as possible, and soon it will become one of the most natural tools in your networking arsenal.

Work the Room

tip #12

To be successful at working the room, you need to be moving around the room regularly and avoid being dragged into endless conversations with one or two individuals.

There are lots of people in the room at any given time, and it is easy for you to get stuck with one person for too long, and miss out on meeting the other people because you are afraid of being impolite when trying to break away from the person you are currently in conversation with.

The important thing to remember is that

networking is about meeting as many people as possible, and nobody should expect you to stay in one place talking to them for hours on end.

Once you have spoken to someone and learned enough about them to move on, you can end the conversation by expressing you delight at having met them, and by saying that you hope to speak to them again soon. You can then offer them your business card if it seems appropriate, and shake hands as you part ways to go and meet other people.

It is also a good idea to remember that many of the people you meet will also have the intention of networking, so you could say something to suggest that you should part and go and meet other people, and rest assured that it won't be taken as an impolite gesture.

Learn

Networking would be completely pointless if you did not take every person you come across as an opportunity to gain information,

You should try and absorb as much information as you can while networking, as this will ensure that your time is well-spent, and that you haven't just met all of the people that you've met in vain.

Everyone you come across and try and network with will have vasts amounts of information that may be vital to your success, and this is indeed one of the most crucial aspects of networking.

You cannot be expected to remember everything you hear throughout the event, because that would be an enormous amount of information; you can, however, keep a notepad at hand to ensure that you do not forget anything important.

You can't take out your notepad and take down notes while talking to someone, though, and that is why its important to listen attentively and be genuinely interested in what the next person says to you, since that will help you to retain all of the important information in memory until you part ways.
Once you part from someone, you make quick notes about anything important that you have learned from them, and you can rest assured that nothing will be lost as you move on to meet someone new.

What About You?

One of the most crucial things to remember when you prepare to start networking with people is that you need to portray yourself in the best way possible, and you need to be able to tell people as much about you as possible in a short time.

One of the most important aspects that you want people to remember about you is your business and the services that you offer, so you need to be able to passionately explain what you do in a way that is brief but still explains all of the important things.

The best way to go about preparing for this is to think about your business or your services beforehand, and write down a complete, but concise, description of everything that your business entails.

It would pay to memorize this description and practice saying it in a casual conversation, so that it doesn't seem forced when you say it to people you meet for the first time.

You need to be extremely enthusiastic when talking about your business so that you can inspire the people you come across to want to do business with you and show them that you are confident about the quality of the services that you have to offer.

Be Yourself

One of the worst things you can do when networking is to try and put up a front to try and convince people that you are a certain way when you aren't.

Many inexperienced people think that they need to pretend to be someone else to fit in and build relationships, but this way of thinking is completely absurd, because it only leads to disappointment in the long term.

One of the most important things you will discover as you gain more experience in networking professionally is that each and every person you come across is an individual with his or her own way of thinking, background, opinions and ideas, and you cannot fake being someone they will get along with.

At some point, you will be found out and this will cause you to lose any credibility that you may have built up with the people that you have befriended, and you could gain a reputation as being someone who is not trustworthy, costing yourself and your business a hard knock in this regard.

Realizing that you cannot please everyone and that there are always people who share the same interests that you do and have the same or similar ideas and passions as you do, is the pivotal step that you need to take in order to overcome the compulsion that you may have to put up a front when networking.

Embrace Technology

At some point on your networking expedition you will find that there are still so many people out there who could potentially be great contacts to have on your network, but you just don't have the time and capacity to go and and meet them.

It is at this stage that you will come to realize that today's technology is truly a wonderful thing, especially for the professional who wants to improve his network in the way that you do. There are so many advancements available today that make extending your network easier than it ever was.

Social networking sites (such as linkedin.com), online organizations, email, VoIP; these are just some of the most popular methods that can be used to increase your network and stay in contact, and with technology constantly changing and improving, it is essential for the success of your networking that you embrace the latest developments and stay current.

More and more people are starting to realize that you don't have to know much about hardware and software to be able to make use of the latest technological trends in networking, all you need to know is the basic operation of a computer and how to access the Internet. The rest is pretty much straightforward or can be explained to you easily.

Networking is all about gaining information and building strong relationships, and in our information age this process can be vastly accelerated and more streamlined and simple than ever before. Online networking is also great for people who are somewhat shy, as it helps them to realize that people are just individuals like them with needs and desires, and this helps them to open up to the many possibilities of networking.

Choose Events Wisely

When choosing which events to go to while expanding your network, you need to remember that you have limited time at your disposal, so you won't be able to attend every single event that may be a networking opportunity. You will have to choose which ones are the most convenient and have the most potential for successful networking.

In oder to make an informed decision when it comes to which events to attend, you need to think about what the goals are that you have in mind when networking, such as expanding your client base, gaining support for a certain aspect of your business, or simply spreading the word about you and your company.

Once you have your goals clearly defined, you can begin to think about which events are most relevant to your networking goals, and which events will attract the most people who are relevant to your networking aspirations, and with these two aspects taken into account, you will be able to eliminate the events which overlap the ones which you definitely need to attend to achieve your networking goals.

You need to remember that eliminating events is not a necessity if you have a lot of time on your hands, it is merely a means to fit in your formal networking if you have a busy schedule or find yourself trying to attend more functions than you have capacity for. If, however, you have enough time on your hands, then it is wiser to view every opportunity as a chance to expand your network and 'work the room'.

Conversation - Ask Open-Ended Questions

tip #18

There are many traps that inexperienced people fall into when the time comes for them to lead or engage in conversation, and one of the most common of these is the fallacy of asking questions that are not open-ended, meaning the question demands nothing more than a simple 'yes' or 'no'.

Asking questions that can be answered in one word is one of the worst things you can do if you are trying to get a conversation going, or hold the attentions of someone that you have just met, since there is nothing to keep them interested once they have answered you and nothing to make them feel like you are interested in anything that they are passionate about.

For this reason, you need to ask open-ended questions that not only expects more than just one-word answers, but demands that the person cannot answer with anything short of a paragraph or at least a full sentence which gives you scope for a follow-up question.

The same is true in the converse situation - do not be the victim of a situation where someone who you want to speak to has asked you a closed question where you can only answer 'yes' or 'no'; be sure to add something to your answer or be ready with a follow-up question that seamlessly leads from the topic that was being discussed.

The point, ultimately, is that you do not in any way want to allow conversations to be led into a dead end so that you and the people you meet are left staring at the floor with nothing more to say to each other. You want to keep the conversation going with a consistent flame so that you are able to transition easily from any topic into something relevant to your goals.

Be Organized

As a networking pro you will be meeting lots of people on a regular basis, and with each person you meet you will be gaining large amounts of information at a rapid rate.

The only way to ensure that none of this information gets lost and that you are able to take advantage of it all as much as possible, is to be organized in everything you do, in the way in which you take notes and how you categorize your information, where you store everything and so forth.

Categorizing information is a vital tool in organizing everything as it helps you to easily store and retrieve any information you might need at any time. You could have categories such as prospective clients, people to meet, upcoming events, attended events and so forth with detailed information stored under each category. For example, under attended events you could list all the events you attended, who you met there and anything significant that you need to remember about the occasion or important conversations that you had.

Whenever you organize anything with regard to building your network, you need to ensure that you have your goals clearly defined and memorized so that everything you do is in line with your goals; so even when categorizing, you need to remember your goals and categorize your information according to your goals.

Speeches

One of the best ways to 'work the room' is to give speeches at the event or function and it can benefit your network in many ways if you do it correctly.

The main reason why it is important to give speeches is that it helps people to remember you, especially if you've introduced yourself to them beforehand and had some kind of conversation.

Speeches also give you the opportunity to speak about yourself, your business or your area of expertize, and conveying the message that you are an expert in any particular field gives you an enormous amount of credibility that could otherwise have taken weeks or even months for you to build up among your network of associates.

When planning to give speeches, however, you should be aware that you are putting yourself on the line and cannot afford to be seen in a negative light at this stage, so you have to be sure that you are comfortable with speech-giving in terms of being able to deliver without showing any anxiety and knowing how to address a large audience and keep their attention.

The best thing to do if you aren't sure about your capabilities is to take a course on speech-giving techniques or at least read up on it on the Internet, and practice your skills with friends or family beforehand to ensure that you are comfortable enough with giving speeches.

Be Open

tip #21

People are generally most comfortable in the company of someone who is completely transparent, and conversely they are quite uncomfortable when they have to speak to someone who isn't open at all.

Transparency means that what you see is what you get, there are no hidden agendas or feelings, and you are someone who can be spoken to easily about almost any topic; most importantly, that people know exactly what they can expect if they were to approach you in any matter.

Being open does not mean that everyone has to know every single detail about your life, merely that there should be no surprises in terms of the type of person you are what they can expect if they need to come to you for anything; this means that you will be seen as someone who is approachable and will go a long way in terms of giving you a good reputation among other people with similar interests.

If you are not sure about whether you are transparent enough, you could ask one of your close friends or family members to help you, perhaps they could tell you about their impressions of you when they first met you, and why they thought you were a certain way in the beginning so that you can work on any shortfalls you may have in this regard.

Find Pro Networkers

One of the easiest ways to fast-track your networking success is to become acquainted with professional networkers who are experts at the networking game and already have a large amount of acquaintances in their own network.

You may think that finding these people is one of the greatest hurdles that you will have to overcome, but in fact it should be quite easy to do because professional networkers will have built up a great reputation among their peers, and a great reputation spreads quickly and spreads in such a way that even people who are new to networking will hear about it.

Another hurdle you may have thought of is that it may be hard to become an acquaintance of the professional networker, but you have to remember that if they follow the same networking etiquette that you do (and they have to follow it in order to be professional at it), then they are constantly looking for more acquaintances to increase their network, and will be glad to meet you and share insights.

Once you become associated with a few professionals, you are that much closer to achieving your goals, and you can be assured of regular expansion in your network of peers as your new associates befriend more and more people.

Have Fun

Some people think that networking is a formal tool used by small business owners or employees to gain the interests of important people and create more sales, but this is far from the truth and an idea that could lead to the failure of any networking exploits before it has even begun.

Networking is not merely about growing your client-base. It should be about making friends. When you network with the aim of making friends you will find an amazing increase in your client-base without you even thinking about it, and this is why networking should be fun, not formal.

While you always maintain a somewhat formal disposition in terms of showing respect to everyone you come into contact with and so forth, you need to make networking a pleasant experience for yourself because this will in turn create a pleasant experience for those you come across.

With a mindset focused on making friends (with clearly defined goals always present in your subconscious), networking will soon become something easy and effective that you can do at any time, and you will find that your influence extends beyond your expected reaches, because your vast network of friends will be the ones to bring you more and more opportunities on a regular basis.

Share

tip #24

Networking and 'working the room' is all about being able to share with other people - share your thoughts and ideas, share your passions and don't forget to share your network with others.

Exchanging networks with people is one of the easiest ways to expand your own. Share at least five names and numbers with someone and they will be glad to share fifty with you, as long as you share selflessly and make an effort to show that you are genuinely interested in helping them.

You have to remember that the vast majority of the people in your own network are themselves avid networkers, so they will be glad to share with you and expand their own networks; which will actually further expand your own network while you build on newer contacts and relationships.

In this way you will also be the first person they come to when seeking new contacts, and so further reinforce your reputation as a great networking resource, which means that more and more people will hear about you and want to share their own networks with you.

Other networkers will also be eager for new thoughts and ideas, and this is why sharing is so important - it gives you a chance to be resourceful and also to gain information and ideas from your network of peers, which is one of the ultimate goals of networking.

"I'm Sorry To Bother You"

As a beginner in the art of building up a social network, you should be mindful of one of the most common fallacies committed by beginners - being "sorry to bother".

Many first time networkers think that they are a bother or that they are interrupting people when they approach someone with the idea of building new relationships, but this is such a negative mindset to have and it could make you come across as a vulnerable and naive person when you approach someone saying *I'm sorry to bother you.*

In this matter, it is vitally important to remember that YOU are a very important resource (whether currently or in the future), and any person who you come across should be (and generally will be) quite glad to make your acquaintance because they are constantly in search of new opportunities; remember that you are not the only person networking.

Once you realize that you are as much an asset to everyone else as someone who you deem to be significant or important may be to you, you will automatically acquire the confidence needed to approach anyone and start building a rewarding relationship from the word *Hello*.

Identify Your Passions

tip #26

One of the best things to do when you are trying to identify things to talk about when connecting with people is to identify your passions. Do so before you begin interacting with others with the intent of networking.

There are a number of reasons why this is an essential and effective step to take in order to network effectively, the first being that when you are truly passionate about something, it not only comes across clearly when you speak about it, but it can be extremely infective in the way your passions can rub off on people because it may make them see things in a new way, the way you see them, and this is a great asset to have at your disposal.

Identifying your passions is also a great way to find like-minded people in a room full of complete strangers; by talking to people about things you are passionate about you will be able to identify which people have similar passions because they will share the same enthusiasm for the subject as you do, and you will notice this immediately, as opposed to those who don't share the same passions as you and those on whom your passions rub off after you've spoken about it.

The only thing to look out for when talking about your passions to people is that, although enthusiastic and passionate about the topic, you should not allow yourself to come across as overzealous and naive, as many people tend to do when discussing something that they are truly passionate about. This is because people tend to regard you as immature or inexperienced if you tend towards being overzealous. Be passionate, but set boundaries for your passion at the same time.

Connect Using Food

One of the best ways to connect with various people in the room is to make use of food - the most natural and effective conversation starting tool in the world.

It is natural that at some point during an event you will need to eat, and there is no reason why you shouldn't take the opportunity to meet new people. All you need to do is ensure that you do not badger people while they are busy eating or while they have food in their mouth. Instead, wait until they have done and take the time to eat your own food, and then speak to them.

Food also makes for a great conversation starter or ice breaker once you have finished the meal. Something like *wow, wasn't that a great meal?* is enough to get a conversation going, and from there you can introduce yourself and start opening up various topics of interest to talk about.

Many people make the mistake of sitting at a table and only eating with the people they already know, but this is a complete waste of a great opportunity to network with some new people. Go and sit at a table full of complete strangers and connect.

The Correct Use of Humor

Humor is a great tool in any conversation, and is especially useful when connecting with new people, but there are also negative factors associated with using humor in your networking endeavors.

One of the most important things that you need to bear in mind is the fact that not everyone can be funny. This is just a fact of life and if you aren't one of the people who knows how to be truly funny, then you should leave humor to the people who do know how. Note the word 'truly' because some people think that they are being funny when really they are not.

You may also use humor in the form of retelling a funny joke that you have recently heard or read. In this case, the same reasoning should apply, although you need not necessarily be a funny person to be able to correctly convey the humor in a joke. One thing to note, however, is that a joke may seem funny to you while it really isn't funny to most other people, so to avoid an awkward situation you should determine whether the joke really is funny or not, and socially acceptable.

In either case you should be absolutely certain of the value of the humor you intend to use before trying to use it on strangers; perhaps by practicing on family and friends and taking into account their reactions.

Avoid Degrading Others

One socially fatal mistake made by many novice networkers is talking about other people's mistakes or bad fortune, and this should be avoided at all cost if you want to be successful at working the room.

Sometimes people fall upon hard times or make mistakes that can cost them their reputation, and often others are quick to take up the opportunity to try and make themselves seem superior in some way by spreading the word or even spreading false rumors of the mistakes of these people, but there are many problems associated with doing so.

One of the most obvious is that you will gain a reputation as being someone who is quick to gossip about others and their misfortunes or mistakes, and this is a very bad reputation to have because it not only makes people very self-conscious in your presence or makes them weary of the things they tell you, but also can cause many people to distrust you because of the connotations associated with gossip-mongers.

Just remember that you are also human and everyone makes mistakes, and you wouldn't want everyone to know about every single mistake that you have made in your life. Most of all, remember that you have enough to offer and therefore have no need to play on the shortcomings of others to get yourself noticed or get ahead.

Remember My Name!

tip #30

There is nothing more valuable to someone in a conversation, especially with a new acquaintance, than having you remember their name.

It is all too common for people to go into a room full of people, start connecting and socializing, and starting up a conversation with someone for the first time. They introduce themselves to the next person and the person tells them their own name, but two seconds later they have forgotten each other's names already, or one remembers (perhaps because he read this tip!) while the other forgets.

The problem is that if you should come to a point in the conversation where you will need to refer to the person by name and have forgotten it, the person may feel severely wounded by it, and besides feeling like you aren't really interested in them or what they have to say, you may lose any bit of credibility that you have built up with the person.

It isn't possible to remember the name of every single person you come across, but that's why it is important to take notes after meeting new people and staying in contact with them. Because people want to be remembered, if nothing more, than by their name.

Grant Success to All

tip #31

One of the greatest reputations you can have if you want to be known for anything, is to have the reputation as someone who brings success to everyone you come into contact with.

The only way you can get this kind of reputation is by truly doing your best to ensure the success of every single person you acquaint yourself with, and not resting until you do so. Even if you don't succeed in this endeavor, but manage to only improve the success of most people you meet, you will become known by more and more people as someone who brings success.

Once you have attained this reputation, more people will want to befriend you than ever before because they will think of you as someone who can bring them success, and in this way success will also come to you.

This is also a really great way to build up relationships with people. Of course if you bring success to someone you will pretty much become their new best friend; but beyond this they will also do whatever they can do to help you attain success, and with so many people helping you it is impossible not to succeed.

Learn from Others

tip #32

The easiest way to become extremely successful in networking is to learn from people who have been doing it for a long time.

Most people you come across will be more than happy to share their knowledge and experiences of networking with anyone, and you should not be to proud to acknowledge that you could do with some help in this regard. The funny thing is that everyone needs help, even people who have years of experience can learn new ways to improve their networking endeavors.

You should also be mindful of the people you learn from. Don't listen to the tips and hints you get from strangers without thinking about whether or not it makes sense, and rather get help from people you know and trust. If you do not know anyone yet, ask your friends or someone close to you whether they think that something makes sense or not.

The best way to learn is to share your own knowledge - in this way you will be able to learn whether others do things differently and figure out whether or not your methods are ideal or if there are more effective methods available.

Don't Sacrifice Your Values

You should never think that you need to let go of your values or principles in order to get ahead, because not only is it not worth it in the long run, but it could earn you a very bad reputation.

We have all come across the concept of a woman who is known as being successful, but at the same time it is well known that she has slept with every single man she has ever come across to reach her success, and the names people call her behind her back are the most horrid names you could think of. Whatever morals, values or dignity she may have had when she first started out in the world has by this point been sold to the devil named 'Success'.

The point here is that, just like this hypothetical woman, many of us are tempted to allow our morals and values to take a back seat in the hopes of impressing someone who we deem to be important in some way; it just is not worth it, though. Often change is a good thing, but sometimes, as in the case of someone who has sacrificed their values for success, change can be extremely negative because it can change the person completely - the way they speak, the way they act, the way they live and even the way they think about things.

The reason for this negative change is that when you first push your principles aside for the sake of success, you get a nagging feeling inside yourself telling you not to do what you're doing. You ignore this feeling, and then ignore it again the next time, forcing the feeling away until eventually the feeling does not appear anymore, and you find yourself losing yourself to a world where you didn't think you would ever be; a world where you and your morals no longer exists.

Learn to Compliment

Once you master the art of delivering a welcomed comment to people you come across you will truly unlock the ability to become a successful networker.

People love being complimented, even if you simply compliment their clothes or style, the way their hair has been done, or any other little thing that not everyone tends to notice, or doesn't say anything about even if they do notice it.

The point is that people want to be noticed, and they want to be noticed in a positive way, and if you can fulfill this desire then you, a complete stranger, have already taken the first step to building a great relationship with them; because everyone loves to be appreciated, no matter how small or insignificant the appreciation may seem to you at the time.

When complimenting people, though, you need to be tactful, not overzealous or allowing yourself to overcompensate, since doing either of these things will ruin the moment and you might as well have introduced yourself with your pants down, because your compliments are meant to make people feel good, not make them uncomfortable.

To ensure that you don't make this mistake, when you think about complimenting someone first ask yourself whether it is an appropriate statement to make to a complete stranger, perhaps imagine that someone you have never met before comes up to you and says this compliment to you and from there determine whether or not it's an acceptable remark.

Rank Your Contacts

At some point when your network of contacts has reached the level where it is hard for you to keep in contact with everyone as often as you would like to so, you may need to rank your contacts.

Ranking contacts allows you to categorize everyone in terms of how important it is to keep in touch with them regularly, allowing you to determine whether certain people can be contacted monthly instead of the usual weekly calls, or quarterly instead of monthly, and so forth.

Categorizing your contacts has many benefits, and it is a fast and efficient way to make sure that everybody gets contacted as and when necessary instead of having to wrestle with the impossible task of trying to contact each person on your network as often as you contact everyone else.

This system is also easy and streamlined, because if someone should at some point require more frequent calls, you simply move them into a higher category, and the same goes for someone who does not need to be called so often anymore.

In this way you can schedule everything accurately without the concern that you have left anyone out, because you will always have a list of people that are due for a phone call or email at any given time, allowing you to ensure that you keep everyone happy and commit enough time to building relationships with those people with whom it is necessary.

You're Allowed to Disagree

tip #36

Nobody likes to talk to someone who disagrees with every single statement that they make during a conversation, but nobody wants to talk to someone who agrees with everything they say either, agreeing as though they don't have their own opinions.

The point here is that you should not be afraid to disagree with someone if you do not feel the same way about something important. Everyone is unique in that they have different view points and different feelings about many different topics, and you need to be comfortable enough with yourself to be able to express yourself if you do not agree with someone on a specific subject.

At the same time, you should not come across as someone who is obnoxious or arrogant. Do not disagree with everything someone says just for the sake of disagreeing with them. People will become very cautious of talking to you if you make a habit of doing this. If you disagree with something that someone says, but you realize that it isn't an important subject and is actually rather petty, there is probably no point in disagreeing.

What it comes down to is that you need to exercise your own logical thinking to determine when it is appropriate to disagree with someone, or when it is better to let it pass and keep your opinions to yourself. You need to strike a balance.

Acknowledge and Paraphrase

When you enter into a conversation with someone who has a lot to say, you need a mechanism for showing them that you are listening to what they have to say, and even more than that, that you are interested in it.

To do this you need to not only acknowledge in whatever way you choose, but also paraphrase what you have heard, and this has many benefits apart from showing the speaker that you are actually listening to what they are saying.

One of these benefits is the fact that if you paraphrase what you heard and say it back to the person who spoke first, you will have the opportunity of conveying your understanding of what was said and allow them the chance to correct you if you misunderstood them in any way, and this has the added advantage of ensuring that everyone in the conversation is on the same wavelength and there are no misunderstandings between you.

Paraphrasing does not mean rewrite in your own words the way you would have done back in high school; it merely means that you should sum up what the person has said and in a very concise manner confirm whether that is what the person actually meant or if they meant something else by what they had said.

You also need to remember that acknowledging what is being said should not merely involve you saying *yes* or *mmhm* all the time. You should mix it up every now and then, make an occasional comment and do the paraphrasing feedback so that the other person never has the chance to feel like you are getting bored by listening to what they have to say.

Know your Industry

When networking it is quite common to come across opportunities where you will be able to speak about what you do and about your business or the business you work for, and if you want to be seen as a professional you need to know your industry.

To know your industry does not mean merely that you know what your own business does and what makes them good at what they do, it also means knowing about your competitors and your target market, as well as substitutes and complimentary goods and services associated with your industry.

You also need to stay current in terms of knowing the latest trends either within your industry or which affects your industry in any way, and if you fall short of this in any way you might find yourself lacking some credibility while speaking to potential customers or people who could have brought you some business.

It isn't hard to stay current with your industry. Most companies have an intranet system, a blog, message board or other similar system for keeping their employees updated about current events that affects the industry, so all you have to do is make sure you check these systems regularly, and staying aware of the news headlines can't hurt either.

These days it is so easy to get information that you need that you don't even have to watch the news or read a newspaper, you can just sit at your desk, open up a web search and type in a keyword related to your industry along with words such as 'latest news' or 'latest trends' and you will be instantly shown thousands of pages and topics related to your industry.

Fish for Topics

It is said that someone who is good at holding long and meaningful conversations is nothing more than a really good fisherman, able to catch big fish with little to no effort.

The reason for this is that every person you come across has a large ocean of topics that they would like to discuss with someone, and all you need to do is to fish for it and you'll have them hooked.

Fishing for topics is not about asking the person what they would like to talk about. They would probably look at you in an odd way and then turn and walk the other way thinking you are just looking for conversation for the sake of it. Instead, you need to find out what they are interested in by listening to them, listen to the things they say, listen to the way they speak and the opinions expressed or not expressed while they are speaking.

When you truly listen to somebody speak, it is as though you can see every single topic they may be interested in discussing floating around about their heads, and it is simply a matter of paying enough attention to ensure that you grab the opportunities to bring up these discussions before they become distracted by something else or before the conversation dies.

A Smile and Warmth

There are few things that make a person more interested in speaking to you than when you have a smile on your face while speaking to them and convey a feeling of warmth and attention at all times.

Smiling while speaking is the simplest thing to do, because a smile should come naturally and not be forced on to its audience in any way. Even if you have had a terrible day, you should not allow it to show on your face because it will make people weary of you. They will get the impression that you are that type of person because seeing you for the first time they probably won't stop to think that maybe you just had a bad day.

Your smile need not be a big, exaggerated smile that is clearly just there for the sake of it. Instead you should try and relax yourself and allow yourself to be in a genuinely good mood, no matter what may be on your mind, because you are going to be connecting with people and you want them to see you on your best.

When you speak with a smile you also seem to come across as someone who is extremely confident, and this will show through so much that people will be eager to talk to you when you approach them; who wouldn't want to be approached by the most confident person in the room?

Beyond all of this, a smile is something that is extremely contagious. Smile at one person and they will infect everyone else with that very same smile until every single person in the room is in a better mood, making it that much easier to connect with anyone and everyone that you have planned to speak to.

Made in the USA
San Bernardino, CA
15 October 2013